SONGS SIGNS AND STORIES
by John Horton

Designed & Illustrated by Michael Kennedy

Pupil's Book Two
ED 11410A

T0081261

Schott & Co. Ltd, London
48 Great Marlborough Street
London W1V 2BN

B. Schott's Söhne, Mainz

Schott Music Corporation, New York

© 1984 Schott & Co. Ltd, London

ED 11410A

ISBN 0 901938 62 9

ROCKS, STONES AND ECHOES

Stones were not only among man's earliest tools, weapons, and building materials, but also some of his first musical instruments. When chipping, breaking, and shaping stones for his own purposes he heard what seemed like voices coming out of them, and sometimes their shapes reminded him of human beings or animals. In time strange legends grew up around the sounds and shapes of stones.

An ancient Greek story tells how Deucalion escaped, like Noah, from a mighty flood that destroyed all the other inhabitants of his country. With his wife Pyrrha, Deucalion floated in a ship over the flood for five days and nights. When the waters began to go down again the ship rested on Mount Parnassus. Deucalion and Pyrrha prepared thankfully to begin life again on dry land, but they felt lonely with no other human beings around them. They asked the gods for help, and were told that Deucalion must throw 'his mother's bones' over his shoulder. This seemed a strange and disrespectful thing to do, until Deucalion realised that by 'his mother's bones' the gods meant the stones that lay all around on Mother Earth. He and his wife then picked up handfuls of stones and threw them over their shoulders. Those that Deucalion threw turned into men, and those that Pyrrha threw became women, so that the land was soon peopled once more.

Another legend describes how two kings, twin brothers named Zethus and Amphion, ruled over the city of Thebes, and planned to surround it with a strong wall. Zethus was a good workman, and was soon dragging heavy stones into place for his part of the wall. Meanwhile, Amphion seemed to be doing nothing but sitting still and playing quietly on his lyre (a stringed instrument). Zethus began to scoff at his lazy brother, until he realised that the music of Amphion's lyre was causing the stones to move by themselves and take up their positions, so that Amphion's section of the wall was finished first.

A third story is about a wood-nymph named Echo. She was a talkative girl, and so much annoyed Hera, the queen of the gods, with her constant chatter that Hera changed her into a rock. After that poor Echo had to keep silent until someone spoke to her, and even then she could answer only by repeating the last word or two that she heard. Another version of the story says that Echo fell in love with a young man called Narcissus, but he was interested only in gazing at his own reflection in a woodland pool, so that Echo gradually pined away with sorrow until nothing but her voice was left.

3

Instruments of stone

The simplest way of using stones to make music is to knock them together, as the native musicians of Hawaii do; they use pairs of lava-pebbles, called *ili-ili*. In Ethiopia large slabs of stone are used as church bells. In Vietnam there are complete sets of sounding stones, chipped until they give the right notes which are laid out on the ground or on a stand and played as if they were xylophones. In ancient China large flat L-shaped stones with a ringing sound were hung on frames and solemnly struck during temple worship or at court ceremonies. The Chinese believed that the voices of the stones could call up the spirits of their ancestors.

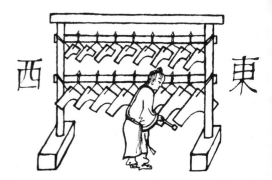

One piece of Chinese music is said to be at least three thousand years old. It was played on various instruments, including stone chimes, when the Emperor entered in procession:

4

THE EMPEROR'S PROCESSION

Drums and wood blocks

Some interesting stone instruments were made in England and can still be seen in museums at Keswick, in Cumbria. They are made from slabs of a particular kind of rock found in the mountain region of Skiddaw. One of the instruments was put together by a stone-mason named Richardson, who worked in the mountains and noticed the musical sound of the stone when he struck it with his hammer. He began to collect suitable slabs and trim them, and after thirteen years he had enough to arrange in rows like the black and white keys of an enormous piano. He and two of his sons then learnt to play pieces of music on the instrument, sitting side by side with a beater in each hand. They gave many concerts, and were invited three times to play to Queen Victoria.

Echoes

We can understand how the legend of Echo grew up. A smooth rock-face or cliff will often throw back any loud sound made near it, and if words are shouted the last word or two will seem to be repeated faintly. The same thing can happen in a cave, a tunnel, or a large building with plenty of empty space, such as a cathedral or covered swimming-bath. We now know that the echo is caused by reflection of the sound, very much as a mirror or pool of water reflects objects near it. Before the scientific explanation was discovered it must have seemed as though someone else was there, repeating the sounds.

It is fun to play echo-games with musical sounds. One singer can echo another, like this:

Now let the first voice, or 'leader', go straight on without waiting for the echo, so that the two voices overlap. The last bit of echo can go on after the 'leader' has finished, but it makes a more interesting sound if they finish together, holding on to their notes when the 'leader' reaches the end of his scale. This holding-on is marked with a sign called a pause (⌢). The sounds are held by both partners until one of them gives an agreed signal to stop the singing:

6

doh te lah soh fah me ray doh

doh te lah soh fah me

Using echo in this way is really the same thing as singing a round. We have already had several rounds; here is another one, with very suitable words. Two, three, or four voices can take part. The second voice gives the first a bar's start, the third follows after another bar, and so on:

LOUDLY PLAY
AND SWEETLY SING

Loud-ly play and sweet - ly sing to

make the hills with e - cho ring.

Sometimes a phrase in a song is repeated like an echo, but
without any overlap. This happens with the first and last
phrases of each verse of 'Cocky Robin':

COCKY ROBIN

1 Who killed Coc-ky Ro - bin? Who killed Coc-ky Ro - bin?

'I', said the spar-row, 'with my lit - tle bow and ar - row, It was

I, it was I.'

2 Who saw him die?___ Who saw him die?___
3 Who caught his blood?___ Who caught his blood?___
4 Who made the cof - fin? Who made the cof -fin?
5 Who dug his grave?___ Who dug his grave?___
6 Who preached the ser - mon? Who preached the ser - mon?

(2) 'I', said the fly, 'with my lit - tle ti - ny eye.___
(3) 'I', said the fish, 'in my lit - tle sil - ver dish.___
(4) 'I', said the crane, 'with my lit - tle nar-row plane.. } It was I, it was I.'
(5) 'I', said the crow, 'with my lit - tle spade and hoe.___
(6) 'I', said the swal - low, 'as loud as I could hol-loa.

Things to do

1 If you live near the sea or among mountains you may be able to find stones that give musical sounds when struck. If you cannot get suitable stones, try old roofing tiles, which usually have holes already drilled in them and so can be hung in a row like the Chinese stone chimes.

2 Find out from books on Egypt about the great statues or colossi of Memnon, which 'sang' when the stone was warmed by the morning sun. Find out also about 'singing sands'. These occur in various parts of the world; in Britain some of the best known are at Studland Bay in Dorset, near Nevin in North Wales, and on the island of Eigg in the Hebrides. An explanation of the sound they make when you walk on them is that they are formed of millions of grains of smooth rock. As these rub together they vibrate and each grain makes a tiny squeak.

3 Find out if there are any echoes in places near your home or on your holidays. A famous echo in a building is the Whispering Gallery of St Paul's Cathedral. Another London building that used to have an echo is the Albert Hall. It was difficult to hear music there, because the powerful echo made the sounds of an orchestra overlap so much, but now some devices looking like flying saucers have been hung from the roof, and there is less echo.

4 If you are interested in science, you can study other kinds of echo, such as:

Living creatures, like bats and dolphins, which are believed to find their way by means of echoes;
Echo-sounding for measuring the depth of the sea and for locating objects like submarines;
Radio echoes, radar, and radio satellite transmission.

5 The story of Deucalion and Pyrrha can be made into a mime with sounds to go with it. The sounds might illustrate:
water the rain splashing, waves rising and sinking, the boat moving on the sea.
wind storm increasing and tossing the boat, then dying down again (voices imitating the noise of the wind).
voices of human beings and of the gods (magnified through cardboard tubes or metal funnels).
stones the rocky landscape, and the throwing of the 'bones' of the earth.

9

THE F SCALE

A scale with F as *doh* fits neatly on to the stave, but to make it work out we have to use a new sign. Suppose we start the F ladder from the top, and go downwards. The four highest steps are easy:

F E D C
doh te lah soh

We want a semitone from *doh* to *te*, and we have it, because F—E is one of the 'white semitones' on the piano. The problem comes with the next two steps as we go down, because C—B also is a 'white semitone', and we don't want a semitone in that position. The place where we must have a semitone is at the *next* step, where the sound ought to be *fah-me*. The way we solve the problem is to push that B down and make a new note, called B flat:

C B A   C Bflat A

B flat is a black key on the piano, and the xylophone and glockenspiel need extra bars for it. From B flat down to A is only a semitone, so now everything is in order, and we can write the whole scale with both its semitones in their right places:

F E D C Bflat A G F
doh te lah soh fah me ray doh

The flat sign ♭ is really a small letter b with a point at the bottom. B was the first note ever to be flattened in this way, but now the sign is used to make any note a semitone lower.

If we are going to use F as *doh* for any length of time we put a flat on the B line at the beginning. This acts as a key signature, and need only be written once for every line of music.

TODAY THE FOX
WILL COME TO TOWN

The word 'town' in this song means somewhere in the country with a farm or a few houses near one another. It is not really a hunting song, but a warning that a fox is on the prowl. Everyone must 'keep' or watch out for him, and drive him off with shouts before he can steal the poultry.

There are two places in the tune where notes are joined together with a curve, like a short slur: These are *tied notes*. The first is three beats long, the second two beats, and they are sung as one long note lasting five beats altogether.

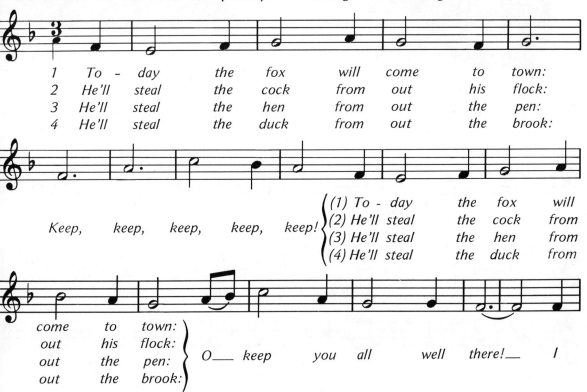

1 To - day the fox will come to town:
2 He'll steal the cock from out his flock:
3 He'll steal the hen from out the pen:
4 He'll steal the duck from out the brook:

Keep, keep, keep, keep, keep!

(1) To - day the fox will
(2) He'll steal the cock from
(3) He'll steal the hen from
(4) He'll steal the duck from

come to town:
out his flock:
out the pen:
out the brook:

O— keep you all well there!— I

must de - sire you, neigh - bours all, To hol—loa the fox from

out of the hall, And cry as loud as you can call:

Whoop! whoop! whoop! whoop! whoop! And cry as loud as

you can call: O— keep you all well there! —

THE MOON

Before trying this Japanese children's song, play an up-and-down ladder on a xylophone, glockenspiel, piano, or recorder:

C D F G A C D C A G F

Now count how many different letter-names you have played. (The high and low C's of course count as only one letter, and so do the two D's.) Think what notes you would have to put in to make the ladder into an ordinary F scale.

This is a scale with no semitones — no *me-fah* (A-B flat) or *te-doh* (E-F). We call it a *pentatonic scale,* and we often hear it in music from lands in the far east, like Japan and China. The whole song is made out of these five sounds, and so is the companion tune (marked *Instruments*) which can be played as an accompaniment.

Instruments

Voices

1 Great is the moon that
2 Great is the moon that

13

looks at me! She's ne-ver ol—der that I___ can
looks at me! Great sun's__ sis-ter she sure-ly must

see. She grows round, it is quite true; some-times
be. Mir-ror-round, and some-times, too, like a

she is ve-ry new. Spring and sum-mer, autumn and
comb of sil-ver curled. Spring and sum-mer, autumn and

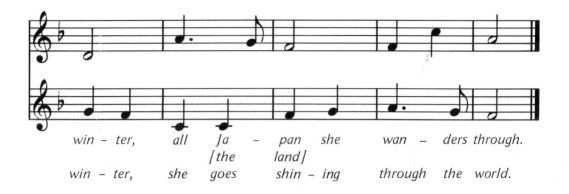

win - ter,   all Ja - pan she   wan - ders through.
          [the   land]
win - ter,   she goes   shin - ing   through the world.

WHEN THE
STORMY WINDS DO BLOW

This fine old song about the life of a sailor belongs to the days when British sailing-ships and British seamen were becoming known all over the world. It can still mean a great deal to us in modern times if we remember the perils and excitements of the fishing fleets, the North Sea oil rigs, and lonely voyages in sailing craft.

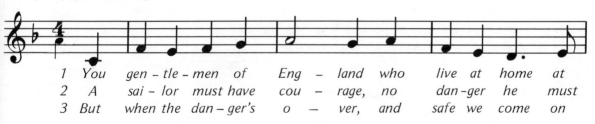

1 You gen - tle - men of Eng - land who   live at home at
2 A   sai - lor must have cou - rage, no   dan - ger he   must
3 But when the dan - ger's o — ver, and   safe we come on

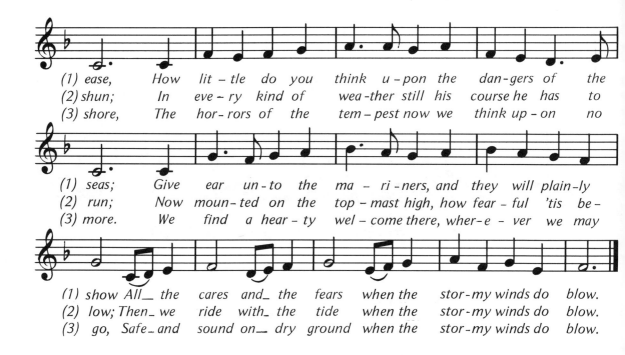

(1) ease, How lit – tle do you think u – pon the dan-gers of the
(2) shun; In eve – ry kind of wea -ther still his course he has to
(3) shore, The hor- rors of the tem – pest now we think up – on no

(1) seas; Give ear un -to the ma – ri -ners, and they will plain-ly
(2) run; Now moun- ted on the top – mast high, how fear – ful 'tis be-
(3) more. We find a hear - ty wel – come there, wher-e – ver we may

(1) show All__ the cares and_ the fears when the stor-my winds do blow.
(2) low; Then_ we ride with_ the tide when the stor-my winds do blow.
(3) go, Safe_ and sound on__ dry ground when the stor-my winds do blow.

Things to do

1 Practise making the flat sign, putting it on the *middle* line
of the stave so that the line shows through the sign:

With this key signature we know that F is *doh*, B flat is *fah*,
and D is *lah*.

2 Fit out a glockenspiel, xylophone, or set of chime bars with the five notes C, D, E, G, A, and an extra C and D at the top:

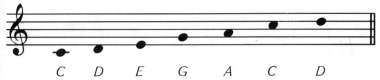

C   D   E   G   A   C   D

From this scale, which is pentatonic (only 5 *different* note-names), you can make up tunes that suggest the music of far-eastern lands. Here are the beginnings of two melodies some of the first European travellers to China heard there and tried to write down. Later they brought them back to Europe, where some famous composers borrowed them to use in their own music:

TUNE A

TUNE B

3 An easy way of finding a ready-made pentatonic scale is to play on the five different black keys of the piano, without touching any of the white ones.

4 Here are two old American songs from the mountains of Kentucky. Work out the letter names of their five different notes, and then practise singing and playing them:

17

PHILADELPHIA

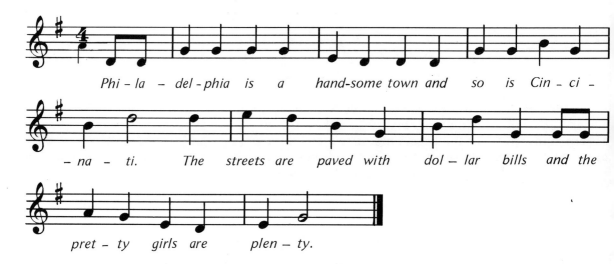

Phi – la – del – phia is a hand-some town and so is Cin – ci –
– na – ti. The streets are paved with dol – lar bills and the
pret – ty girls are plen – ty.

OLD BALD EAGLE

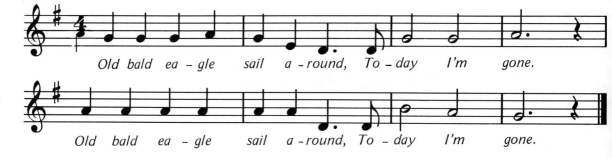

Old bald ea – gle sail a – round, To – day I'm gone.

Old bald ea – gle sail a – round, To – day I'm gone.

THE GUARDIAN OF THE WINDS

Among the many adventures that befell the warrior Odysseus and his men on their voyage home after the siege of Troy was their meeting with the Guardian of the Winds. They landed on a floating island with a great wall of bronze around it. The ruler of this island was named Aeolus, and the gods had entrusted to him all the winds that blow. Aeolus treated the wanderers kindly, and with his large family of sons and daughters, entertained them royally for a whole month. When they were ready to leave, the king put into the hold of Odysseus' ship a leather bag fastened with a silver clasp. In this bag Aeolus had shut up all the winds except a gentle western breeze which would waft the ship homewards to the island of Ithaca.

They sailed on peacefully, with all sails set, for nine days and nights, until they could see the shores of Ithaca. Soon they were so close that they could make out the wisps of wood-smoke rising from the house-tops, and Odysseus lay down contentedly to sleep on deck. But while he rested, the crew began to murmur among themselves. That leather bag in the hold, they said, must surely contain gold and silver, and they wanted their share, as they had been with their master through all his wanderings and hardships.

At last they agreed to unfasten the silver clasp and find what was inside. The moment they did so, all the winds rushed out together, the waves rose high around them, the ship was blown back and forth, and they were rapidly carried out to the open sea and back to the island kingdom of Aeolus. The Guardian of the Winds was astonished to see them, for he thought he had done all he could to bring them safely home. Odysseus tried to explain how his crew had opened the bag while he slept, and he begged Aeolus to forgive them and help them again.

19

But Aeolus was both angry and afraid. Odysseus, he said, must have offended the gods in some way to bring this misfortune on his head, and it would be dangerous to help such an unlucky man.

There was nothing for it but to set out once more. This time there was no gentle wind to waft them, but only a dead calm, and the crew had to toil night and day at the oars. After six days' hard rowing they reached unknown land where they hoped to find food, water, and shelter. But it was inhabited by cannibal giants who hurled rocks at the ships to sink them, and then carried off the drowning men to devour them. Only Odysseus and a few of his men escaped, and they had to go through more perils and sufferings until Odysseus, alone of all his crew, drifted on to the shore of Ithaca.

Things to do

1 Read more of the adventures of Odysseus (or Ulysses).

2 See how many words you can find to describe the movement and sound of gentle and strong winds.

3 Find out how the strength of winds is measured on the Beaufort scale.

4 Collect sayings and rhymes connected with the wind. Here is one to start with:

When the wind is in the north
the skilful fisher goes not forth.
When the wind is in the south
it blows the bait in the fish's mouth.
When the wind is in the east
it's good for neither man nor beast.
When the wind is in the west
it's then it's at its very best.

5 Find out about a strange musical instrument named after the Guardian of the Winds. It is called the Aeolian harp, and is made by stretching strings or thin wires across a frame and fixing it in an open window, so that the wind can blow upon the strings. There is no tune, but a mysterious humming as several strings vibrate at the same time.

It is something like the sound made by telegraph wires or overhead electric cables when a strong wind makes them vibrate.

6 Try some of the experiments that follow, to discover how air vibrates and makes musical sounds.

1 Pull out the handle of a bicycle pump as far as it will go, put your thumb firmly over the valve hole so that no more air can enter or escape, and push the handle back as hard as you can. Then release the handle, making sure that the valve hole is still firmly covered. What do you notice? What do you think this experiment shows about air?

2 Blow across the end of a cardboard tube, and listen to the sound it makes. Do the same thing again, but this time cover the bottom end of the tube firmly with the palm of your hand. What difference have you made to the sound?

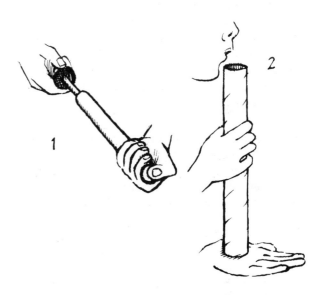

3 Blow across the ends of plastic straws (or real straws if you can get them: oaten ones are best) until you get a clear sound. Then try cutting the straw to shorten it, and notice how the sound changes.

4 Blow across the open end of a milk or mineral water bottle and listen to the sound. Then pour a few inches of water into the bottle and notice how the sound changes. Try this with different amounts of water.

21

5 Take several bottles of the same size, arrange them in a row, and check that they all make the same kind of sound when you blow across them. Then pour a different amount of water into each bottle until you have a scale. As a change from blowing, try tapping gently on the top rim of the bottle with a wooden kitchen spoon.

Warning: if you tap the *sides* of the bottles, or use glass tumblers instead, you will spoil the experiment, because you have turned the glass into a kind of bell, which obeys different laws.

6 Take off the top joint of your recorder and blow gently into it. Then put it back into its place, use the fingers of both hands to cover all the holes of the recorder, and blow again. Now take your right-hand fingers away and listen to the sound when only the left-hand holes are covered.

7 Make a buzzer by rolling a square of thin but strong paper diagonally round a pencil. Fix the roll with a bit of sellotape and slip the pencil out. You will now have a pipe with a small triangle at each end. Cut one of the triangles very carefully so that you can fold it like a flap over the end of the pipe. It must fit close, but be free to move up and down. Put the flap end into your mouth, close your lips but not your teeth, and blow gently. The flap should begin to vibrate and the pipe will make a buzz. (Don't be discouraged if this does not work at first. It helps if the flap is moistened slightly.)

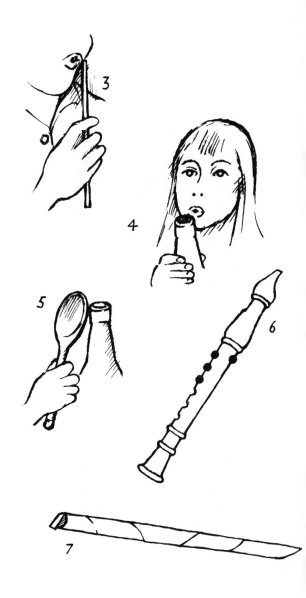

22

What we have learnt from the experiments

1 Air is springy or 'elastic'. Although it is invisible, it can be squeezed like rubber and bounces back again.

2 The air in a tube can be made to vibrate in several ways: by blowing across one end, by blowing through a narrow opening on to a sharp edge in the 'window' of the recorder, or by making a tongue or 'reed' vibrate.

3 A closed pipe, blocked at one end, sounds an octave lower than an open pipe of the same length.

4 The shorter we make the column of air or 'speaking length', the higher the sound.

5 The more air there is to vibrate in a narrow bottle, the lower the sound. Adding water fills up some of the air space.

WILL KEMP'S DANCE FROM LONDON TO NORWICH

William Kemp lived in the reign of the first Queen Elizabeth. He was the clown or comic actor in some of Shakespeare's plays, and could make the audience laugh the moment he came on to the stage. He was also a fine and athletic dancer. Besides dancing in the theatre as part of his act, he undertook long-distance dances, earning both fame and money from wealthy people who sponsored him and from the crowds that gathered along the roadside to watch him. He was famous not only in England, but also abroad in Germany, France and Italy. His greatest feat of endurance was to dance the morris, a lively and strenuous dance popular at that time, all the way from the City of London to Norwich. It took him nine days altogether, not counting the time for resting, meals, and sleep. He wrote an account of his journey in a little book called *Kemp's Nine Days' Wonder*, with a picture of himself in embroidered jacket, wide breeches, a hat with a large feather, scarves hanging from his arms, and bunches of little bells tied to his legs. Beside him in the picture marches his companion, Thomas Slye, playing music for the morris dance on a three-holed pipe and a tabor or small drum.

Here is a diary of Kemp's dance from London to Norwich:

First day He started at seven in the morning one fine Monday in early spring from the Lord Mayor's House in the City of London. Three men were with him — Thomas Slye with his pipe and tabor, George Sprat who acted as 'overseer' or referee to see that Kemp took no extra rests, and a manservant, William Bee. Hundreds of people had turned out to see them start, and many of them threw money to encourage them. Kemp danced along Whitechapel to Stratford, Mile End, and Ilford, where he politely refused a drink out of the Great Spoon of Ilford which held a quart of liquor. At Romford he spent two days resting at an inn; he was glad enough to have got there in safety, as just outside the town he was nearly trampled under the hooves of a pair of runaway horses.

Second day Thursday began badly, for Kemp strained a muscle, but cured it simply by going on dancing, and so got to Brentwood, where it was market day. The streets were crowded, and two men were caught picking pockets. They pretended they were officially collecting for Kemp's dance, but when Kemp assured the authorities that he had never set eyes on the rogues before they were punished and sent back to London, where they had come from. Kemp then danced on to Ingatestone. It was now nighttime, but about fifty people still followed him by moonlight.

Third day (Friday) The crowd had grown to about two hundred as Kemp set out in the morning for the large town of Chelmsford. It took him more than an hour to push his way through the people and to reach his inn, and by that time he felt so exhausted that he could not dance another step. So he spoke to the waiting crowds from his bedroom window, and explained that being in training he could not accept any of their invitations to dinner. But he soon began to get over his weariness, and kindly allowed a girl of fourteen, who seems to have been the local junior champion, to dance the morris with him in the largest room of the inn. She managed to keep up with him for a whole hour, until Kemp was obliged to confess that the strongest man in Chelmsford could not have done so well. He took a weekend rest until Monday.

Fourth day The way from Chelmsford to Braintree was long and muddy, with thick woods on both sides and deep holes in the road. Two country lads tried to join in Kemp's dance, one of them just ahead of him and the other at his heels. At last they came to a puddle so wide that Kemp had to take a flying leap at it, reaching the other side up to the ankles in dirty water. One of the youths trying to follow him fell right in the middle of the pool and had to be rescued by the other. After that they left Kemp to go on by himself to Braintree, where he rested for two nights.

Fifth day Wednesday's stretch took him to Sudbury, in Suffolk. A burly man, a butcher by trade, offered to keep him company as far as Bury St Edmunds, but after only half a mile he also dropped out, saying he could not keep up if he were offered a hundred pounds. Another young girl appeared, however, borrowed some of Kemp's bells to tie on her legs, and actually stayed the course as far as Long Melford. There Kemp was met by a gentleman named Mr Coles, who took him to his house and entertained him from Wednesday night until Saturday morning.

Sixth day Mr Coles's household jester danced along with Kemp for part of the way from Long Melford to Clare, and later a wealthy widow invited Kemp to her home and gave him a splendid meal. At last he reached the great town of Bury St Edmunds in the afternoon. At that very moment the Lord Chief Justice of England happened to be entering the town through another gate, but Kemp was proud to find that it was his dancing, and not the Chief Justice's procession, that attracted the largest crowds. Unfortunately the weather changed, and Kemp had to stay snowed up in Bury until the following Friday morning.

Seventh day This was Friday in the third week of Kemp's journey. By now the snow was thawing, and he made good progress from Bury across the heath (now called the Breckland) to Thetford, covering the ten miles in three hours. As it was assize time, Thetford was more crowded than usual, but a gentleman named Rich was true to his name, let Kemp stay in his fine house for two days, and then sent him on his way with a gift of five pounds.

Eighth day (Monday) The next stop was an inn at Rockland. The innkeeper was so proud of having a famous visitor like Kemp that he put on his best suit of clothes and began to make a speech in his honour. But the poor man was overcome with nervousness, and all he could stammer out was: 'Master Kemp, you are as welcome as — as the Queen's best greyhound'. The innkeeper even tried to accompany his guest as far as Hingham, but was much too fat to keep up with the dance. The local youths and girls kept offering to show Kemp the easiest way through the slushy lanes.

Ninth day Now came the last stage of the journey. From Hingham, by way of Barford Bridge, Kemp arrived at the city of Norwich. But it was hopeless to try and dance through the crowd that thronged the streets, and Kemp decided to ride in on a borrowed horse, though he knew that to keep the rules made for him he would have to do the morris through the streets later on.

So he rode into the market place, where the city musicians or 'waits' were all ready, wearing their silver-gilt chains and holding their instruments with red and white silk banners attached, to play in Kemp's honour as they had played for the Queen herself a few years earlier. Kemp thought these Norwich musicians were as good as any in the country, and later wrote in his book:

'Besides their excellence in wind instruments, their rare cunning on the viol and violin, their voices are admirable, every one of them able to serve in any cathedral church as choristers.'

Will Kemp knew that the Mayor and Corporation were waiting in the Guildhall, dressed in their furred robes, to give him a civic welcome, but the crowd pressed so closely round him that the horse could not move. So he jumped off its back, skipped over a low church wall, and found another way into the Guildhall. In the meantime the 'overseer', George Sprat, had completely lost sight of Kemp among the crowd, and insisted that the last bit of the journey would have to be done all over again. But by this time the Mayor and Corporation were receiving Kemp with every honour Norwich citizens could offer him. He was given five pounds in gold on the spot, and a pension of forty shillings a year for life; he was made a

Freeman of the Merchant Venturers' Company; and the boots in which he had come all the way from London were solemnly hung on the walls of the Guildhall. And so ended Kemp's Nine Days' Wonder.

Will Kemp's Music The three-holed pipe to which Kemp danced was something like a small recorder, but much harder to play, as all the notes of the tunes had to be made with the first two fingers and thumb of the left hand, while the other left-hand fingers held the pipe between them and the right hand beat the tabor to mark the time.

Kemp knew how to play the pipe and tabor himself, but when dancing he had to leave it to Thomas Slye. We do not know what morris tunes Slye chose to play on the famous nine days' journey, but we can make a good guess at some of them. We know that Kemp was fond of the tune called 'Trenchmore', which is the one we have already sung to the words 'Today the fox will come to town'. The tune on this page has words mentioning Kemp and some of the usual figures in the morris when it is danced by a team:

SINCE ROBIN HOOD

Since Ro-bin Hood, Maid Ma-ri-an, and Lit-tle John are gone-a, The hob-by horse is___ quite for-got, when Kemp did dance a-lone-a.

Another tune, called 'Watkin's Ale', also has words that refer to Kemp's exploits abroad. The words stop after the first eight bars, but we have printed the whole tune, which is quite long, so that you can play all of it if you like.

WATKIN'S ALE

He did la-bour af-ter the ta-bor for to dance then

in-to France.

Last of all, here is a tune known as Kemp's Jig. There are a few signs in it that we have not come across before. The empty-headed note without a stem **O** is a *semibreve*, and must be held for four whole beats. The tune is in the G scale, and therefore has an F sharp key signature, making nearly all the F's into F sharps. But in two places the F sharp is 'cancelled' by means of a sign called a *natural* (♮). In those places we play F and not F sharp. Soon afterwards the sharp is put back again. Then, just once, there is a B flat. Notes which do not really belong to the key we are using, but crop up occasionally, are called *chromatic notes*. These particular ones, F sharp and B flat, are quite easy to play on the recorder.

KEMP'S JIG

The Betley Window

32

Things to do

1 Make a map of Kemp's journey from London to Norwich, and find the distances between some of the places mentioned in the story. A motoring road book will help; the roads do not run quite the same as they did in the time of Elizabeth I, but Kemp's route was roughly along the present A11, A118, A12, A131 and A134.

2 Find out more about the old town musicians or 'waits'. Those of Norwich who played to Kemp were so famous that in 1589 Francis Drake borrowed six of them to take in his ship when he went to Corunna to 'singe the King of Spain's beard' (meaning to set his fleet on fire). A few years earlier another Elizabethan seaman, Sir Humphrey Gilbert, had not only musicians but also morris dancers in his ships when he sailed to Newfoundland to plant an English settlement. The morris dancers were to entertain the sailors and to please the native people and make them more friendly.

3 Learn how to dance some of the morris steps. As we have seen, the dance can be done by one or two persons, but a full team or 'side' was made up of at least eight dancers, some of them dressed to represent different characters. If you examine the picture on page 32 you will see the characters in a full team. This picture shows an old stained glass window in Staffordshire. See if you can find the hobby horse, the fool or jester, the pipe and tabor player, the man dressed as Maid Marian, the Friar, and some dancers with bells on their legs.

33

COUNTING AND NUMBERING

Numbers and figures have a great deal to do with helping us to understand how music is made and how it is written down.

1 Every musical sound has its *frequency* or vibration-number: for example, the note A is made by a string vibrating nearly 440 times in a second. A string that vibrated twice as fast (880 times a second) would sound an octave higher

2 If we want to know how fast to play a piece of music, we sometimes use a metronome to help us. We set the metronome so that it ticks so many times in a minute; for example, if we set it to the figure 60 it will tick that number of times per minute, or once a second. Crotchets played at that speed (♩ = 60) will be quite slow. ♩ = 120 would mean two crotchet beats a second, or twice as fast.

3 We also count to make sure how long a sound has to last, and we can put these different lengths into a kind of multiplication table:

1 crotchet beat ♩

2 crotchets make 1 minim ♩

3 crotchets make 1 dotted minim ♩.

4 crotchets make 1 semibreve 𝅝

We use fractions, too:

half a crotchet beat is   1 quaver ♪

a whole crotchet equals 2 quavers ♫

one dotted crotchet ♩. plus one quaver ♪ makes up 2 whole beats (1½ + ½).
Quarter beats are shown by 4 semiquavers

4 Another use for counting is to find how many bars make up a phrase, and how many phrases a complete tune contains.

5 Then there are the time-signatures, which remind us how the beats are grouped — in twos: $\frac{2}{}$ or threes: $\frac{3}{}$ or fours: $\frac{4}{}$.
(Another way of writing these is $\frac{2}{4}$, $\frac{3}{4}$, $\frac{4}{4}$ or **C**).

6 Another important use for counting is to be able to say how far one sound is higher or lower than the next, or what *interval* they are apart. You can remember the names of the intervals if you learn this amusing little song:

A se-cond, a third, a fourth, a fifth, a sixth, a seventh, an oc-tave.

A se-cond, a third, a fourth, a fifth, a sixth, a seventh, an oc-tave.

7   We use numbers to show fingering. In piano playing the thumbs count as 1 and the other fingers as 2, 3, 4, 5, ending with the little finger. With some other instruments, like the violin, which do not use the thumbs to make sounds, the numbering starts with the index finger and goes 1, 2, 3, 4.

Songs with counting words Most people know a few songs of this kind, such as 'One man went to mow' and 'The animals went in two by two'. Here are some more:

TWENTY, EIGHTEEN

In this we have to count *backwards*, first in even numbers and then in odd numbers. Some of the old country singers liked to have a competition over it, to see who could sing the counting words fastest without making a slip.

1 O yon-der stands a__ char-ming crea-ture,__ Who she is I
2 O Ma-dam, I__ have come to court_you,__ If your fa-vour
3 O Ma-dam, I__ have rings and jew-els,__ Ma-dam, I have
4 O what care I__ for_ rings and jew-els,__ What care I for

(1) do not know; I'll__ go__ court her for her beau-ty,
(2) I may gain; And_ if__ you will en – ter-tain me,
(3) house and land; Ma – dam,_ I have wealth and trea-sure,
(4) house and land? What_ care _ I for wealth and trea-sure?

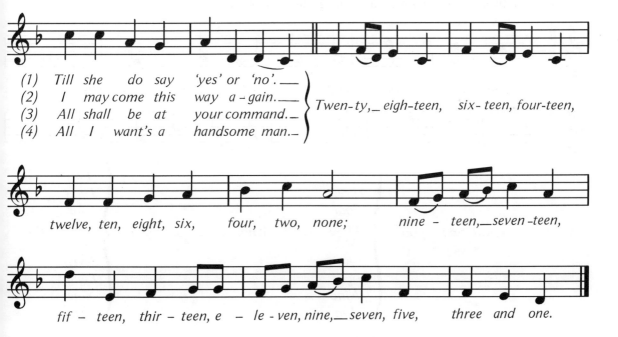

(1) Till she do say 'yes' or 'no'. __
(2) I may come this way a-gain. __
(3) All shall be at your command. __
(4) All I want's a handsome man. __

Twen-ty,_ eigh-teen, six-teen, four-teen,

twelve, ten, eight, six, four, two, none; nine - teen,_seven -teen,

fif – teen, thir – teen, e – le -ven, nine,_seven, five, three and one.

THE DILLY SONG

The counting here is easier, but the words are full of mystery and no one understands exactly what they mean, though they seem to have a great deal to do with ancient legends and religious beliefs. Every verse begins with two questions and two answers, so that it is a good idea to share the song between two people or two groups of singers.

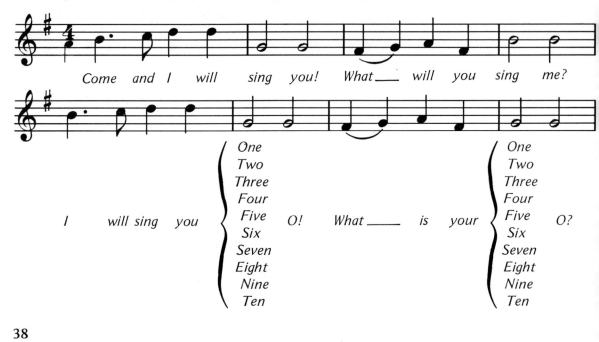

Come and I will sing you! What___ will you sing me?

I will sing you ⎰ One / Two / Three / Four / Five / Six / Seven / Eight / Nine / Ten ⎱ O! What ___ is your ⎰ One / Two / Three / Four / Five / Six / Seven / Eight / Nine / Ten ⎱ O?

1 One   of   them is   all   a - lone, and   e – ver   will   re –   main   so.
2 Two   of   them are   lily-white ba - bies   dres-séd   all   in   green   O!
3 Three of   them are   stran-gers, o'er the   wide world they are   ran – gers.
4 Four   it   is   the   Dil - ly Hour, when   blooms the gil - ly –   flow - er.
5 Five   it   is   the   Dil - ly Bird, that's   ne – ver seen but   heard   O!
6 Six   the Ferry-man   in   the boat, that   on   the ri - ver   floats O!
7 Seven it   is   the   Crown of Heaven, the   shin – ing stars be   seven   O!
8 Eight it   is   the   mor – ning break, when   all   the world's a –   wake   O!
9 Nine   it   is   the   pale moon-shine, the   pale moon-shine is   nine   O!
10 Ten for– bids all   kind of sin, and   then be – gins a –   gain   O!

THE SEVEN HOPS

This Dutch song needs not only counting and singing, but also action. At the word *one* you put your left foot forward, at *two* your right foot; at *three* you put the left foot forward again and bend that knee, at *four* right foot forward and bend that knee; at *five* put your left elbow on the floor, at *six* your right elbow; and at *seven* try to touch the floor with your nose. If you like you can then repeat the song with all the movements in reverse until you are standing straight up again.

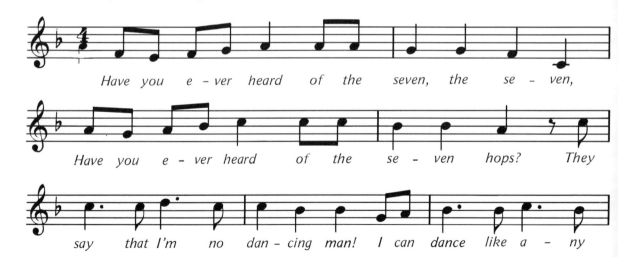

Have you e - ver heard of the seven, the se - ven,

Have you e - ver heard of the se - ven hops? They

say that I'm no dan - cing man! I can dance like a - ny

no - ble-man. That is one! That is two! That is three! That is

four! That is five! That is six! That is se - ven!

UN DEUX TROIS

If you know some French, this song will give you practice in counting up to 12. The word *neuf* means 'nine' the first time it comes, but the second time it has its other meaning 'new' (so that *dans mon panier neuf* means *in my new basket*).

Un, deux, trois, nous i - rons au bois,
1   2   3

quatre, cinq, six, cueil-lir
4   5   6

des   ce - rises,

sept, huit, neuf, dans mon pa - nier   neuf,
7   8   9   [new]

dix,   onze,   douze, elles   se - ront   toutes   rouges.
10   11   12

TEN FINGERS

This is a very easy little song for counting on all the fingers. It is printed here in a scale we have not used before, with A as *doh*. If you experiment, you find that *three* sharps are necessary for this scale — the F sharp and C sharp we have used already, and a new note, G sharp, to make the semitone just below A. In the key signature this G sharp is hoisted into the space right on top of the stave.

One and two, three, four, five,

one and two, three, four, five, six and seven,

eight, nine, ten; Then go back and start a – gain.

Things to do

1 On page 34 are the vibration-rates or frequencies of two of the A's on the piano. See how many other A's you can find on the keyboard, and then work out their frequencies.

2 Find out something about the inventor Mälzel (or Maelzel), who gave his name to the clockwork metronome.

3 Look carefully through the song 'Twenty, Eighteen', and find all these intervals somewhere or other in the tune:

> a *second*
> a *third*
> a *fourth*
> a *fifth*
> a *seventh*

4 The two notes of an interval need not always come one after the other. They can be sung or played so that they sound together. Here is a set of intervals made out of the F scale. Try playing them with a pair of beaters on a glockenspiel or xylophone, or with two forefingers on the piano. Start with both beaters or both fingers on the same note (this is called a *unison*), and gradually widen the interval until you reach the *octave*. Don't forget the B flat.

unison second third fourth fifth sixth seventh octave

5 When you have found all the intervals, and can play them while counting two beats to each, get a descant recorder player to fit the first two phrases of 'Twenty, Eighteen' on top of your intervals; or you can make a piano duet of it, like this:

Player 1

Player 2

SOME NEW TIME-PATTERNS

We have learnt how to divide a crotchet beat into halves, called quavers. We can now think about quarter-beats, called semiquavers. To write a single semiquaver, worth a quarter of a crotchet beat, we simply add an extra tail to the quaver sign:

Four semiquavers, making up a whole crotchet, can have their tails fastened together:

Here is a rhythm-game to be played in three groups, A, B and C:

Group A Clap quietly, steadily, and not too fast:

Group B Tap with a finger on the palm of the other hand:

Group C Tap like Group B, but twice as fast:

It is a good idea for Groups A and B to practise together first, and then for C to join in with the semiquavers. It will help Group C if they whisper the word *se-mi-qua-vers* while they tap.

45

Sometimes a crotchet has to be split into a half and two quarters, or two quarters and a half:

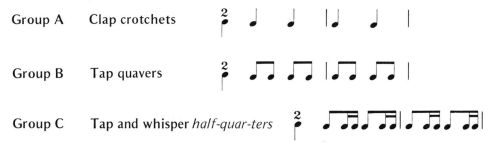

Group A   Clap crotchets

Group B   Tap quavers

Group C   Tap and whisper *half-quar-ters*

When this has worked out right, try it the other way round:

quar-ters-half

There is one more pattern worth practising, because it comes so often in lively tunes. This pattern is made up of three quarters plus one quarter:

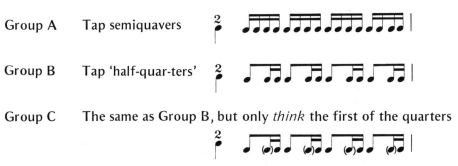

Group A   Tap semiquavers

Group B   Tap 'half-quar-ters'

Group C   The same as Group B, but only *think* the first of the quarters

Group C's pattern is a jumpy rhythm that we usually write like this:

THE JOLLY MILLER

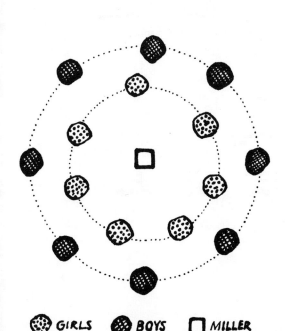

⬤ GIRLS   ⬤ BOYS   ☐ MILLER

We have printed this in the A scale. As you can see, it contains semiquaver patterns. Make up your own percussion accompaniments, using drum, tambourines, cymbals, triangles and any other suitable instruments. Choose any of the time-patterns marked 'accompaniment', or have several of them going at the same time.

'The Jolly Miller' used to be a favourite play-song or party game. An outer circle of boys and an inner circle of girls (one fewer than the number of boys) formed the 'wheel'. The 'miller' stood in the middle of the wheel. The two circles walked round in opposite directions. At the word 'grab' every boy, including the 'miller', tried to catch a partner, and the one left without any had to take his turn as the 'miller'.

Accompaniment:

(etc.)

DAY DAWNS
WITH FREIGHT TO HAUL

This is a dock-workers' song from East Africa, very short but sung over and over again while loading or unloading cargo. The hauling shouts of *e-ya* should be pronounced '*ay-yah*'.

Day dawns with freight to haul: e – ya, e – ya,

Day dawns with freight to haul: Look for the la – bel!

TALL STORIES

This comes from Spain, where no one is expected to take the words seriously:

1 Do you know what I have seen a-long the way I've
2 Do you know what I have seen a-long the way I've
3 Do you know what else I saw as I pur—sued my

(1) come? Three rab—bits in a tree were bea—ting
(2) come? A field—mouse I saw cha—sing an old
(3) walk? Three chic—kens and a vix—en in a

(1) on a drum. O no? O yes! A—long the way I've
(2) cat called Tom. O no? O yes! A—long the way I've
(3) friend—ly talk. O no? O yes! As I pur-sued my

(1) come, Three rab – bits in a tree were bea – ting on a drum.
(2) come, A fieldmouse I saw cha – sing an old cat called Tom.
(3) walk, Three chic – kens and a vix – en in a friend – ly talk.

[After v. 3]:

O no? O yes! But a – ny way, I vow My

stock of these tall sto – ries is all fi – nished now.

Things to do

1 Practise writing semiquavers:

heads first

then stems

then tails

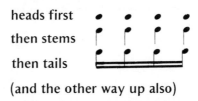

(and the other way up also)

2 Collect more songs with nonsense words, such as 'The Derby Ram' and 'The Crocodile'.

3 Play this old Welsh tune on the recorder, and write out percussion parts to go with it, remembering that it is a march. It is played and sung both in Wales and across the sea in Brittany. Just as many Welsh people speak two languages, Welsh and English, so many of the Bretons speak Breton, which sounds something like Welsh, as well as French.

There is a story that long ago in a war between Britain and France, soldiers from Wales and Brittany found themselves on opposite sides. But when each army heard the other singing the same marching-song, and orders being shouted in nearly the same words, they refused to fight and shook hands.

CAPTAIN MORGAN'S MARCH

(The sets of dots between the spaces of the stave are *repeat signs*, and mean that each pair of phrases should be played twice.)

52

WINDMILLS AND WATERMILLS

Every kind of food-grain — wheat, barley, oats, maize, rye and millet—has to be ground or pounded into meal or flour before it can be baked or prepared in some other way for eating. In some parts of the world handmills are still used; they consist of a flat or hollowed-out lower stone and a heavy upper stone with which to rub or beat the grain. The upper stone often has one or two handles fixed to it so that two people, sitting each side of the mill, can share the labour of turning it. A handmill of this kind is sometimes called a quern. Handmilling was a long wearisome job, and it was generally the women who were expected to do it. To make it go a little more easily they sang as they turned. Here is an old Irish quern song with a pentatonic tune:

THE QUERN TUNE

Maids at __ morn, grind the good__ corn Each in __ her__

mill with a will! In __ go the oats, wheat and pear-ly bar-ley,

Down in __ a shower falls the flour.

Win - ding__ strong, grind-ing all day long, Round, round__ and __

53

round   goes   the mill;   Grind-ing turn a - bout,   till   the meal is   out, must

ne – ver, ne – ver stand   still.

It was probably in eastern lands that men discovered how to use the powers of wind and water to turn huge circular stones and grind enough grain to feed whole villages. Windmills were being used in Arab countries at least a thousand years ago, and in time they were introduced into Greece, Spain, France, and other parts of Europe. Many were built in the eastern counties of England and in the lowlands of Holland, where they were made not only to grind corn but also to pump water out of marshy land.

Watermills too seem to have been invented in the Arab countries. They work by having a strong stream of water pouring on to wooden blades fixed to a large wheel, which is connected to machinery for turning the grinding-stones inside the mill-house. Tide-mills are similar, but are built near river estuaries in order to harness the power of the tides as they ebb and flow. There were at least five thousand water-mills and tide-mills in England by the year 1086, when they were listed in William the Conqueror's Domesday Book. Water continued to be the main source of power for factories (still called 'mills' in northern England) until the invention of the steam engine.

In the Isle of Man there is a glen where a water-mill can still be seen, though it no longer grinds corn. This song was made about it when it was still working:

MANX GRINDING SONG

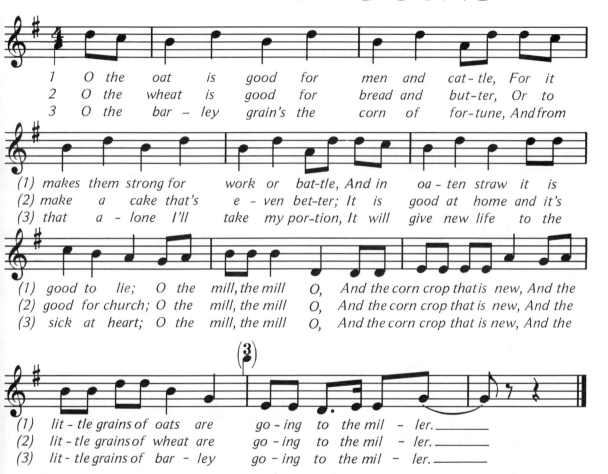

1 O the oat is good for men and cat-tle, For it
2 O the wheat is good for bread and but-ter, Or to
3 O the bar - ley grain's the corn of for-tune, And from

(1) makes them strong for work or bat-tle, And in oa - ten straw it is
(2) make a cake that's e - ven bet-ter; It is good at home and it's
(3) that a - lone I'll take my por-tion, It will give new life to the

(1) good to lie; O the mill, the mill O, And the corn crop that is new, And the
(2) good for church; O the mill, the mill O, And the corn crop that is new, And the
(3) sick at heart; O the mill, the mill O, And the corn crop that is new, And the

(1) lit - tle grains of oats are go - ing to the mil - ler._____
(2) lit - tle grains of wheat are go - ing to the mil - ler._____
(3) lit - tle grains of bar - ley go - ing to the mil - ler._____

The miller used to be one of the most important men in the village, and one of the most prosperous, as his work was useful to everybody. This explains why there are so many songs about him. Some of them describe how he was paid by 'taking toll' — that is, keeping an agreed share of the flour from each customer for his own use; not

55

always fairly, perhaps, but other tradesmen
did the same, if we can believe this French
song:

WHEN THE MILLER
STARTS A-MILLING

1 When the mil - ler starts a - mil - ling, clit - ter, clat - ter goes the mill;
2 When the tai - lor starts a - sew - ing, snip - per, snap - per go the shears;
3 When the wea - ver starts a - weav - ing, jig - ger, jag - ger goes the loom;
4 When the young folks get to - ge - ther, chat - ter, chat - ter go their tongues

(1) Clit - ter, clat - ter goes the mill - wheel round.
(2) Snip - per, snap - per go the shin - ing shears.
(3) Jig - ger, jag - ger goes the noi - sy loom.
(4) Chat - ter, chat - ter go their bu - sy tongues.

(1) From the meal he takes care to have a bu-shel for his share.
(2) From the cloth he takes care to have a mea-sure for his share.
(3) From the wool he takes care to have a bas - ket for his share.
(4) From the news they take care to have some gos - sip for their share.

Another thing that was sometimes said about the miller was that he had a problem finding a suitable wife. An English song and a Dutch one both mention this point. To understand the Dutch song, remember that the sails of a windmill have to be set to catch the wind from whatever direction it happens to be blowing. In England this was usually managed by means of an ingenious 'fantail' wheel, invented in 1745 by a miller named Edmund Lee. The fantail catches any wind and turns the cap or top of the mill, sails and all, in the right direction. In Holland the sails had to be pulled round with a pole fixed to the cap, a chore that might account for the trouble the Dutch miller had in making up his mind.

THERE WAS A MAID
WENT TO THE MILL

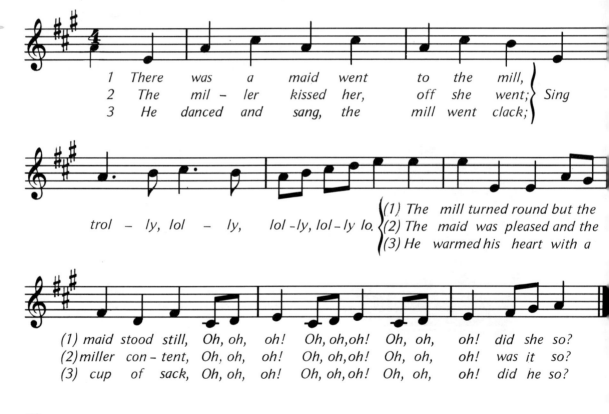

1 There was a maid went to the mill,
2 The mil - ler kissed her, off she went; Sing
3 He danced and sang, the mill went clack;

trol - ly, lol - ly, lol - ly, lol - ly lo.

(1) The mill turned round but the
(2) The maid was pleased and the
(3) He warmed his heart with a

(1) maid stood still, Oh, oh, oh! Oh, oh, oh! Oh, oh, oh! did she so?
(2) miller con - tent, Oh, oh, oh! Oh, oh, oh! Oh, oh, oh! was it so?
(3) cup of sack, Oh, oh, oh! Oh, oh, oh! Oh, oh, oh! did he so?

WHEN THE WIND COMES FROM THE SOUTHERN SIDE

When the wind comes from the { sou — thern / nor — thern / eas — tern / wes — tern } side (with hap-sal-de-

- ra, fal — de-ra), And the mill turns round and the

wind blows { south, / north, / east, / west, } then the mil — ler says { that Rose-ma-ry shall / an — o -ther girl shall / a dif-ferent one shall / the last is best to }

be his bride (with le -rum, la — rum, hap — sa — sa).

✻ *[If the high F is too difficult, sing the lower one.]*

The sound of the machinery, with the chugging of the big water-wheel, has found its way into many mill songs. Here are two: the first, which is very short, is from Czechoslovakia, and the second tells of a contented life in a French mill:

CZECH MILL SONG

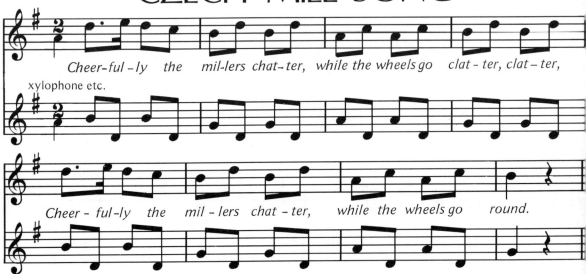

Cheer-ful-ly the mil-lers chat-ter, while the wheels go clat-ter, clat-ter,

xylophone etc.

Cheer-ful-ly the mil-lers chat-ter, while the wheels go round.

60

HARK TO THE MILL-WHEELS

1 Hark to the mill-wheels, what they say: I will be mar-ried
2 I love the mil-ler as my life. Soon, he has said, I'll
3 When all the work is done at last, We'll shut the door and

(1) one fine day. The mil-ler is a fine young man, He
(2) be his wife. He'll grind the corn with all his might, And
(3) make it fast. When we have ea-ten eve-ry-thing, Then

(1) works all the day as hard___ as he can:
(2) then I will get his sup-per eve-ry night: } Round go the mill-wheels,
(3) we'll have a dance and glad-ly we will sing;

tick-a-tick-a-tack-tack, Round go the mill-wheels, tick, tick, tack.

Ioan Stradanus inuent.   Phls Galle excud.

Things to do

1 Find out if there are any windmills or watermills (working or not) in your district, and look out for more when you go on holiday. A large-scale map usually marks them. Some old windmills have been restored and can be visited. There is plenty to learn about the various kinds of windmill — 'tower', 'post', and 'smock', and about the different kinds of sails. Watermills too have different ways of using the water, as the wheels may be 'overshot' or 'undershot'. If you are interested in machinery, you can find out how wind or water power is made to turn the millstones through systems of gears. Then you can go on to find out how milling is done nowadays without the old sources of power (though the principle of the watermill is used in the turbine for generating electricity).

2 Look for more songs about millers, like 'The miller of the Dee', and a North Country ballad, 'The miller and his three sons' which is about toll-taking.

3 The picture on page 62 shows some watermills in Germany several hundreds of years ago. The mill closest to us has been built beside a river, from which water is forced through a narrow opening (notice the little waves) and turns two mill-wheels under the archways. The water-wheels are made of wood, and wooden gears fit into one another and drive round the mill-stones in the room above. Look carefully at the picture and you will see that:
   (a) Each pair of mill-stones is supplied with grain through a kind of trough or hopper.
   (b) Horses or mules loaded with sacks of grain are arriving at the mill.
   (c) The miller is weighing sacks of grain, while another

man (in the window) seems to be writing down the weights in a book. The weighing machine is of the kind called a 'steelyard'.

(d) Two of the miller's men are pouring grain into the hoppers. There is also a boy; can you guess what his job is?

(e) A spare mill-stone, with its grooves, is leaning against the wall outside.

(f) Chickens, ducks or geese, and pigeons belong to the mill. Why are these profitable for the miller to keep?

(g) In the distance are two floating mills, looking like Noah's arks. Why do you think they are kept near the middle of the river? How are they connected to the river bank?

Once upon a time all the trees agreed to choose one of themselves and anoint him as their king.
First they said to the olive tree:

> *Come and reign over us.*

But the olive tree replied:
> 'Why should I give up my rich oil, which is used for honouring God and man, in order to become chief of all the trees?'

Then they said to the fig tree:

> *Come and reign over us.*

But the fig tree replied:
> 'Why should I give up my sweetness and my good fruit, and become chief among the trees?'

Then the trees said to the vine:

> *Come and reign over us.*

And the vine answered them:
> 'Why should I leave my grapes, which give wine for God and man, in order to become chief among the trees?'

Then last of all the trees called to the bramble:

> *Come and reign over us.*

And the bramble answered the trees:
> 'If you really want me as your king, you can come and put your trust in my shadow. But remember that fire can leap out of the bramble, fierce enough to devour the cedars of Lebanon, which are the greatest of all the trees.'

KING BRAMBLE

Things to do

1 This story is taken from the Book of Judges (Chapter 2) in the Old Testament of the Bible. Try to make a series of pictures to illustrate it. They can be coloured or black and white drawings, or they can be pictures in sound.

2 Here are some ideas for sounds:

The trees agreeing to elect a king Heavy instruments, like large drums, can represent the trunks of the larger trees; lighter instruments, like small drums and rattles, their swaying branches; and delicate instruments, like tambourines and triangles, their rustling foliage. Find a rhythm-pattern for the words *'Come and reign over us'*, and use it each time the words occur in the story.

The olive tree Find out all you can about the olive. Its fruit, which looks like green plums, contains oil used for cooking and salad. How can the oil 'honour God and man'? The answer is in the use of oil in religious ceremonies and at coronations. The olive tree is also prized for its beautifully grained wood. Choose instruments with a smooth, gentle sound for the olive (recorders might be suitable) and try letting them play in thirds, perhaps like this:

The fig tree One of the curious things about the fig is that it bears its fruit before the leaves open. What are the leaves like? What colour is the fruit when it first forms, and when it is ripe? The story mentions the sweetness of the fig, so find some sweet-toned instruments to represent it. Chime bars or glockenspiels might do, playing either in thirds, or better still in sixths to distinguish the fig from the olive:

The vine Everyone has seen bunches of green or purple grapes in shops, or even growing outdoors in warm and sheltered positions. Music for the vine should suggest the twisting, slender stems of the plant, its delicate tendrils, and the hanging bunches of fruit. It might also suggest the lively scenes, with dancing, that take place in warm countries when the ripe grapes are being gathered and the wine pressed out. This will mean plenty of quaver or semiquaver time-patterns, including dotted notes, and rhythmic percussion as well as melodic instruments.

The bramble The bramble is able to grow in rough, dry ground and it protects its soft and juicy fruit with prickly thorns. Instruments with a dry, hard sound would therefore be best for the bramble's music: try wooden instruments such as xylophones (played with hard-headed sticks), wood blocks, claves, castanets, and guiros (scrapers). The sound-picture should be full of irregular, jagged noises, and should represent not only the bramble itself but also the fire it threatens. It might make a good ending to the whole piece if all the other trees could join in with their own music, while the bramble sounds try to swallow them up.

Fitting words and sound-pictures together The words of the story can be shared among many voices, all speaking together or separately for the replies of the different trees. The speakers can stop and wait for the sound-pictures to be played, and then go on to the next part of the story. With some practice, the musicians can learn to start just before the speaking voices have finished their sentences, so that the whole story unrolls itself in words and music.

If you are interested in dancing, you could work out a ballet of group and solo dances to illustrate the story.

MORE ABOUT SCALES

By now we are quite used to the scale pattern that has the eight singing names:

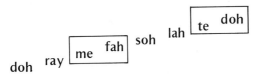

We can always recognise this pattern when we hear it, because of the two semitone steps between *me-fah* and *te-doh*. It does not matter what note we choose for *doh*; the scale will sound right as long as the tones and semitones come in the same order. We have already used these notes as *doh*:

C

G (needing an F sharp for *te*)

D (needing an F sharp for *me* and a C sharp for *te*)

A (needing an F sharp for *lah*, a C sharp for *me*, and a G sharp for *te*)

F (needing a B flat for *fah*)

Now let us add two more scales to the list.

Suppose we try to build a scale with the usual pattern, starting from B flat. We shall soon find that we need an extra flat to make the *me-fah* semitone:

(We start from a low B flat, to make a scale that is comfortable to sing.) The new note is E flat.

Now take this E flat and make it the starting-note; once more we shall have to use a new note, A flat, for the *me-fah* semitone:

To avoid writing these flats each time we need them, we put them as key signatures at the beginning of a piece of music:

doh is F   *doh* is B flat   *doh* is E flat
(*lah* is D)   (*lah* is G)   (*lah* is C)

Rules to learn

If there is no key signature, *doh* is C

If there is a sharp key signature, the sharp furthest to the right is *te*

If there is a flat key signature, the flat furthest to the right is *fah*

Major and minor

Most of the tunes we have sung and played up to now finish with *doh*. We say they are in the *major mode*.

But many tunes finish with *lah*, like this song from Russia:

THE BIRCH TREE

1 Birch-tree, stand-ing there in the mea-dow, Lea-fy birch-tree stand-ing in the
2 Ear-ly will I rise in the morn-ing, Ear-ly will I rise up in the
3 Three small twigs I'll cut from your bran-ches, And three pipes I'll make me for to
4 From a fourth I'll make a ba-la - lai - ka, And I'll strike the strings in sweetest

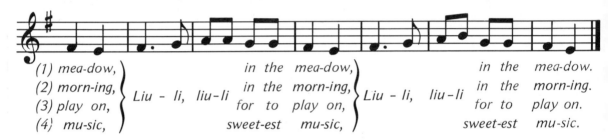

(1) mea-dow,   in the mea-dow,   in the mea-dow.
(2) morn-ing,   Liu - li, liu-li   in the morn-ing,   Liu - li, liu-li   in the morn-ing.
(3) play on,   for to play on,   for to play on.
(4) mu-sic,   sweet-est mu-sic,   sweet-est mu-sic.

These *lah* tunes are in a *minor mode*. They usually (though not always) have a sadder sound than the major-mode tunes. Here is a round, printed with the key signature of one flat which shows that F is *doh* and D is *lah*. There is also an extra sharp (C sharp) to make a semitone step up to *lah*. When this happens we give it a special singing name, *se*:

AH POOR BIRD

Ah, poor bird, take thy flight Far a-bove the sor-rows of this dark night.

70

The round can be sung by two, three, or four groups of voices, each starting the tune when the previous group has finished the first bar (that is, the first three words). Each group should sing the whole tune three times and then drop out.

Minor-mode tunes are not all sad. Here is a very jolly one, from the days before tractors and lorries, when all the farm work had to be carried on by the strength of men and horses. For the heaviest jobs a team of horses was used, and the carter was responsible for looking after the animals and making them understand what to do. Some of the carter's shouts to the horses come near the end of the song. 'Hey' means 'turn right', 'hee' means 'turn left', 'hoo' is 'stop', and 'gee' is 'go on'. This was sometimes used as a forfeit song when work was over for the day and everyone was looking for some amusement. Four different people would then try to give the right shout at the right time, and the one who missed would have to pay for drinks for the others.

'Bears the bell' means 'is the best of the team'.

THE CARTER'S HEALTH

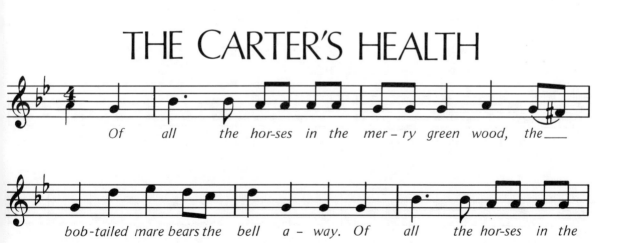

Of all the hor-ses in the mer – ry green wood, the___ bob-tailed mare bears the bell a – way. Of all the hor-ses in the

mer- ry green wood, the bob-tailed mare bears the bell a – way. There is

Hey, there is Ree, there is Hoo, there is Gee, but the bob-tailed mare bears the

bell a – way. There is Hey, there is Ree, there is Hoo, there is Gee, but the

bob-tailed mare bears the bell a – way. Hey, Ree,

Hoo, Gee, but the bob-tailed mare bears the bell a – way.

Things to do

1 Here is a Breton dance tune, arranged for two players. The tune is in the top line, while the lower line has an accompaniment that moves up and down the steps of the minor scale. *Doh* is G, and *lah* (on which the tune begins and ends) is E:

2 These are the beginnings of five major-mode tunes. All are national anthems. Decide what keys they are in, sing or play them, and find what countries they belong to:

(c)

(d)

(e)

3 These are the beginnings of three well-known minor tunes.
See if you can recognise them, and then try to play them
right through:

(a)

(b)

(c)